TREE OF LIFE

TREE OF LIFE

TREE
TALES

The World of the African Baobab

BARBARA BASH

Sierra Club Books | Little, Brown and Company
San Francisco | Boston • New York • Toronto • London

To my parents,
and to all the people who are
fighting to save the vitality
of the African ecosystem

The author wishes to thank the National Museum of Kenva for its
help in researching information for this book.

The Sierra Club, founded in 1892 by John Muir, has devoted itself to the study
and protection of the earth's scenic and ecological resources — mountains, wet-
lands, woodlands, wild shores and rivers, deserts and plains. The publishing
program of the Sierra Club offers books to the public as a nonprofit educational
service in the hope that they may enlarge the public's understanding of the Club's
basic concerns. The Sierra Club has some sixty chapters in the United States and
in Canada. For information about how you may participate in its programs to
preserve wilderness and the quality of life, please address inquiries to Sierra Club,
730 Polk Street, San Francisco, CA 94109.

First Paperback Edition

All calligraphy by Barbara Bash

Library of Congress Cataloging-in-Publication Data

Bash, Barbara.
    Tree of life: the world of the African baobab / Barbara Bash. — 1st ed.
      p.   cm. — (Tree tales)
    Summary: Text and pictures document the life cycle of this
    amazing tree of the African savannah, and portrays the animals
    and people it helps to support.
    ISBN 0-316-08322-4 (pb)
    1. Baobab — Africa — Ecology — Juvenile literature.
    2. Baobab — Africa — Life cycle — Juvenile literature.
    3. Savanna ecology — Africa — Juvenile literature.
    [1. Baobab. 2. Trees. 3. Africa. 4. Ecology.] I. Title.
    II. Series.
    QK495.B7B37 1989
    583'.19 — dc19   89-6028

10 9 8 7 6 5

BP

Sierra Club Books/Little, Brown children's books are published by Little,
Brown and Company (Inc.) in association with Sierra Club Books.

Published simultaneously in Canada by
Little, Brown & Company (Canada) Limited

Printed in the United States of America

In the oldest times, as the !Kung
Bushmen of Africa tell the story,
the Great Spirit gave each animal
a tree to plant. Hyena arrived late
and was given the very last tree,
the baobab. Being a careless
creature, he planted it upside
down—and that is why its
branches look like gnarled roots.

The baobab grows on the dry savannahs of Africa. Reaching crookedly into the air, it stands silent and ancient. Many people believe there are no young baobabs – that they spring into being full grown. Perhaps this is because the young, slender trees look so different from the older ones. They begin to thicken and twist after forty years of growth and can eventually measure up to forty feet across and sixty feet high. With a life span of more than one thousand years, baobabs outlive nearly everything on earth.

Sour Gourd Tree, Cream of Tartar Tree, Monkey Bread Tree, the Elephant of Plants – there are many names for the baobab. The African people also give each old baobab its own special name beginning with "Um," which means Mother. For them, the baobab is filled with mystery, and they honor it like an elder.

For most of the year the baobab
stands leafless and bare, but twice
a year the rains come, and for a
brief period the tree leafs out and
blooms. Sometimes even before the
rains begin, the baobab senses the
coming moisture and sends out
its soft new leaves and flower buds.

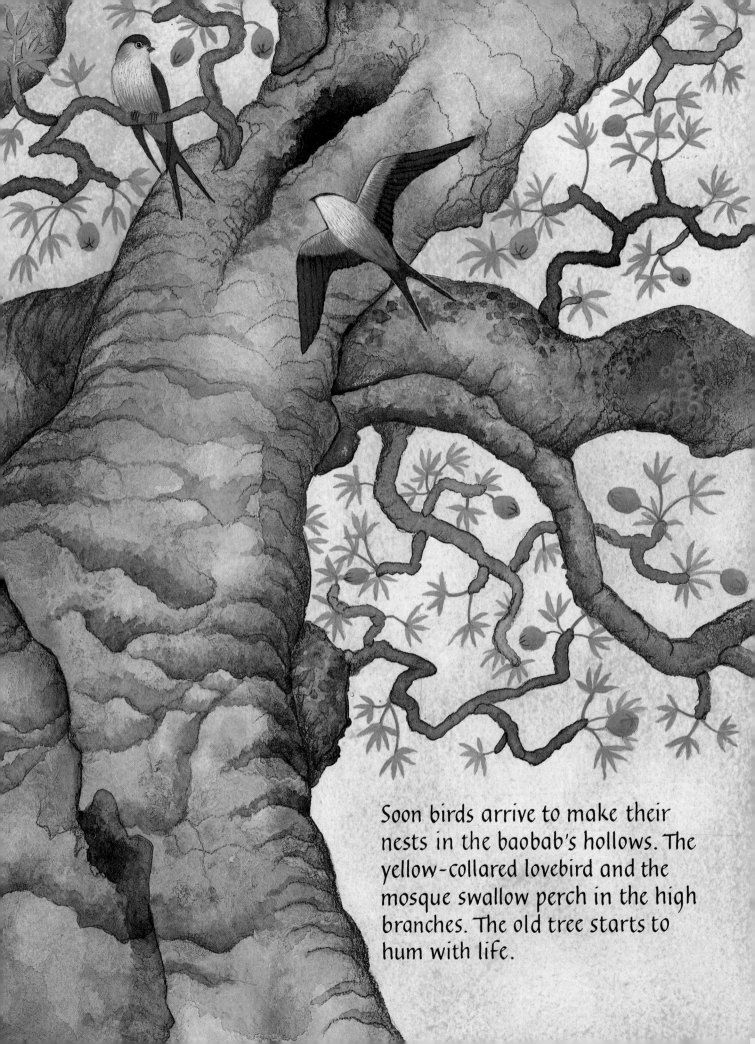

Soon birds arrive to make their nests in the baobab's hollows. The yellow-collared lovebird and the mosque swallow perch in the high branches. The old tree starts to hum with life.

Under the opening leaves, the orange-bellied parrot, lilac-breasted roller, and yellow-billed hornbill also make their homes. Once the yellow-billed hornbill has chosen a hollow in which to lay her eggs, she seals herself inside it with mud. Her mate feeds her insects through a tiny slit for more than six weeks. Then, when the eggs have hatched and the babies are large, she breaks out of her crowded, protective prison. The chicks rebuild the damaged hole and are fed by their parents for three more weeks, until it's time for them to break out and fly.

Sweat bees

Longhorn
beetle

Soon after the rains begin, the
baobab is full of activity. Tiny
sweat bees build slender tunnels
leading to their hives inside the
tree. The cotton bollworm eats the
baobab wood, while the longhorn
beetle, elegant grasshopper, and
Masonga caterpillar munch the
foliage. In the center of the tender
leaves, cotton stainer bugs, flea
beetles, and long-tailed mealybugs
cluster and chew.

Elegant grasshopper

Cotton
bollworm

Long-tailed
mealybug

Flea
beetle

Cotton
stainer
bug

Masonga
caterpillar

At twilight, the large white flowers begin to open. Small furry creatures called bushbabies emerge from their hollows in the tree and smell the sweet nectar. They dart from branch to branch like little elves, pushing their faces into the flowers, lapping up the nectar, and carrying the sticky yellow pollen on to the next bloom. The soft leaves rustle as the bushbabies chirp and scurry about

Deep in the night, the fruit bats
arrive to drink the flower nectar,
too. The mothers fly with their
young pups holding on to their fur.
The restless fluttering goes on all
night. Standing under the dark
tree, one might think there were
spirits in the baobab branches.

In the morning, the flowers that
opened the night before have fallen
to the ground, and a pair of eland
comes to lap up the soft petals.
A trio of impalas also munches the
petals quietly, keeping a watchful
eye on the horizon for signs of
danger. No one seems to notice
the tiny dik-dik that hides in the
lush grass nearby. In the distance, a
lone giraffe reaches for the baobab's
tender leaves.

In a few weeks, the rains end and the baobab's leaves begin to fall, exposing the weaver nests. The male red-headed weaver has been weaving a hanging nest with a long entrance spout at the end of a branch, while the buffalo weaver has built a spiky clump of twigs. Both nests protect the birds' eggs from dangerous snakes. When the nests are complete, the male weavers attract females to the new homes they've built. But if the females don't like the nests, the males must start all over again! The tree is full of weaver nests, and the birds dart busily in and out.

When all the leaves have fallen, the fruit begins to develop. Soon hundreds of big melon shapes hang from the bare branches. Before long, a family of baboons arrives to feast on the fresh fruit.

They spend the whole day in the baobab, cracking open the hard velvety shells and scooping out the sweet pulp of all the fruit they can reach. Seeds fall to the ground as the baboons scamper and chortle.

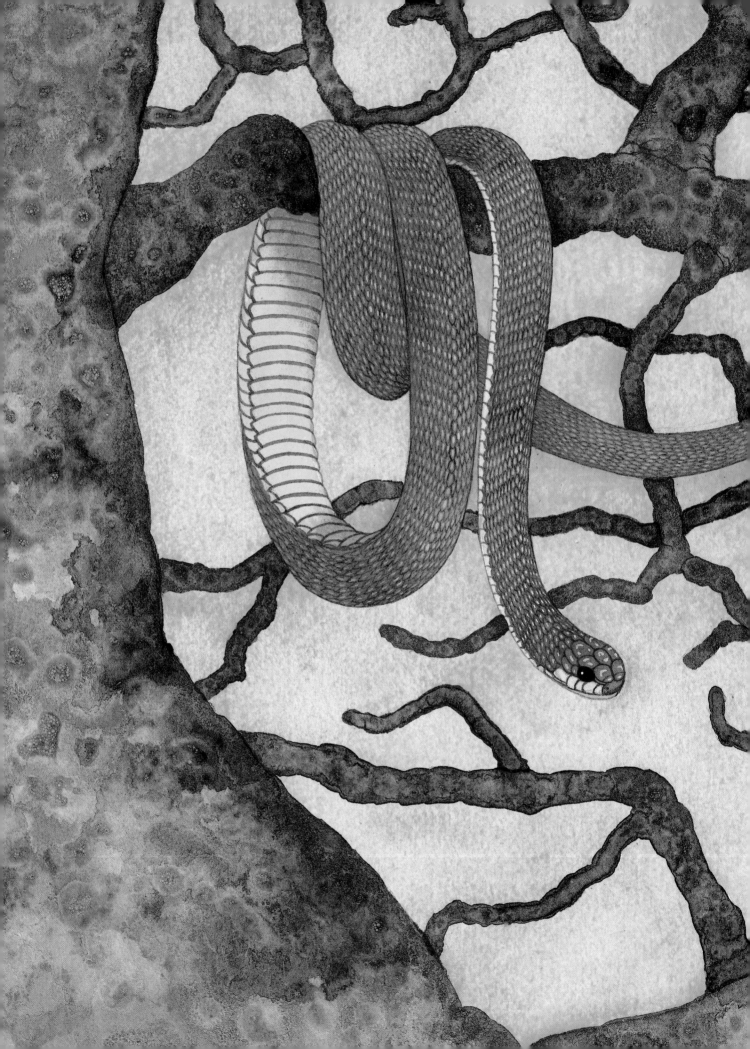

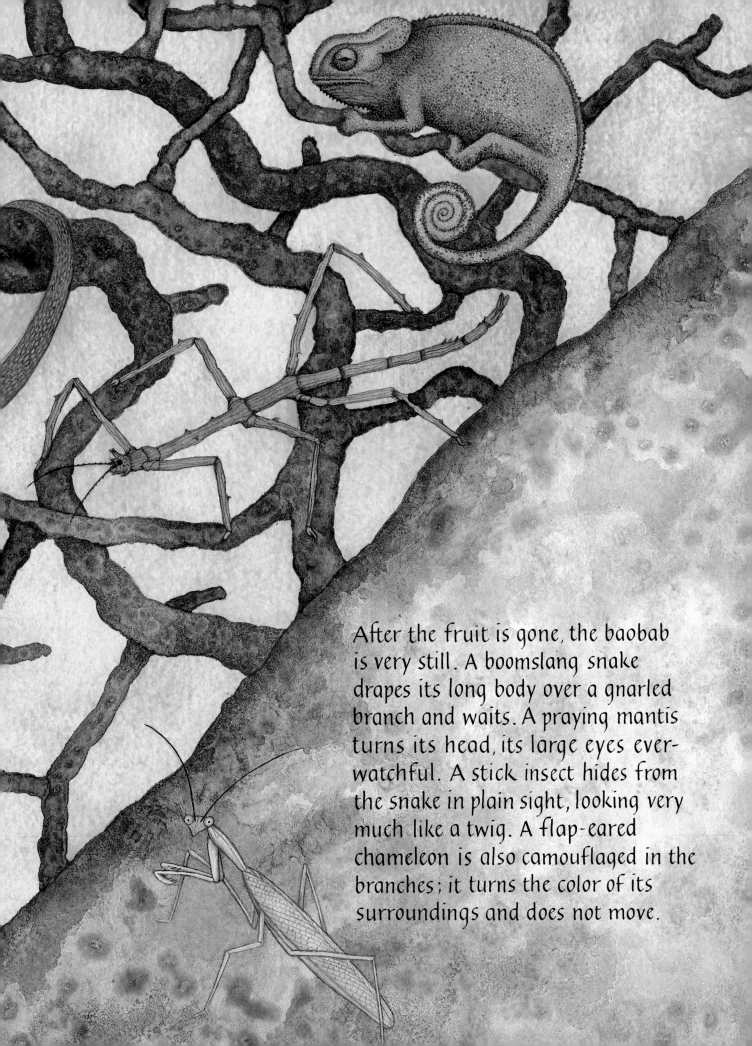

After the fruit is gone, the baobab is very still. A boomslang snake drapes its long body over a gnarled branch and waits. A praying mantis turns its head, its large eyes ever-watchful. A stick insect hides from the snake in plain sight, looking very much like a twig. A flap-eared chameleon is also camouflaged in the branches; it turns the color of its surroundings and does not move.

Sometimes the stillness is broken by the call of the honey guide bird—*aje-je-je-je*—and the voices of tribesmen who follow close behind. The bird dips and swoops, flashing its white tail feathers, until it gets close to a hive in the baobab. Then the honey guide perches quietly nearby and waits for the hunters to find the hive. The men climb the baobab, smoke out the bees, and scoop out the honey. But they always leave some beeswax behind, as thanks to the honey guide bird.

To the African people, the baobab is more than a source of honey. Its bark is stripped for baskets and rope; its fruit is made into candy and sweet drinks; and its roots and leaves are used as medicine. On the hot, dry savannah, the hollow trunks of ancient baobabs can also become water containers and even shelters.

At the end of the long, dry season, the thirsty elephants arrive and begin to eat the baobab bark, extracting juices from the soft fiber. With their enormous strength, the elephants strip away all the bark and pull down large chunks of wood, leaving gaping holes in the trunk. But the baobab heals its wounds, produces new bark, and keeps growing.

Finally, after many, many years, the
old baobab dies. Perhaps too many
elephants have chewed the wood and
weakened its structure, or insects
have broken down its inner core.

One day it collapses in on itself, a
melted heap of ruins. Over time, only
a soft mound of powdery fragments is
left. The wind will blow these away
until nothing of the baobab remains.

In the sky, the clouds begin to build for the coming rains. Near the dust of the dead tree, a baobab seed has sprouted. It is all alone on the wide savannah. Now the story of the baobab begins all over again.

Ten Holiday Jewish Children's Stories

Retold by Barbara Goldin

Illustrated by Jeffrey Allon

PITSPOPANY

NEW YORK ◇ JERUSALEM

Sources:
The Book of Our Heritage by Eliyahu Kitov, Feldheim Pub.
Great Jewish Thinkers: Their Lives and Work by Naomi Pasachoff, Behrman House
The Baal Shem Tov by Zalman Aryeh Hilsenrad, Kehot Publication Society

Published by PITSPOPANY PRESS
Text Copyright © 2000 by Barbara Goldin
Illustrations Copyright © 2000 by Jeffrey Allon

Pitspopany Press books may be purchased for fund-raising
by schools and organizations by contacting:
Marketing Director, Pitspopany Press,
40 East 78th Street, Suite 16D, New York, N. Y. 10021.
Tel: (800) 232-2931, Fax: (212) 472-6253.
E-mail: pop@netvision.net.il
Visit our website at: www.pitspopany.com

Design: Benjie Herskowitz

ISBN: 0-943706-48-3 Softcover
ISBN: 0-943706-47-5 Cloth

Printed in Hong Kong

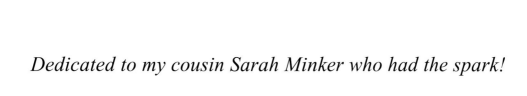

Dedicated to my cousin Sarah Minker who had the spark!

Barbara Goldin

For Moriyah Rute and Shelly

J.A.

ALSO AVAILABLE IN THIS SERIES

Ten Best Jewish Children's Stories

Ten Classic Jewish Children's Stories

Ten Traditional Jewish Children's Stories

Table of Contents

Jewish Storytelling
by Yaacov Peterseil

TELLING A JEWISH STORY SEEMS TO FULFILL, for many of us, some very basic needs. When we open a Jewish children's book we also open a passageway that allows our frustrated other selves to escape, at least momentarily. For example –

The frustrated actor-parent tells a story so as to permit herself to jump, shout, make faces, laugh out loud, and relive those carefree childhood days when it was all right to behave foolishly and clownishly – after all, that's the way the characters in the story sometimes behave.

The frustrated rabbi-parent tells a "learn from this" parable in order to realize his dream of captivating an audience, of mesmerizing with word or gesture those congregant-children who are hearing this story for the first time. Such a parent secretly praises God, saying, "How wonderful it is to impart knowledge. How satisfying to be looked up to. Surely, this is what the prophets felt when they preached their morality sermons to the masses. Halleluyah!"

The frustrated workaday-parent experiences the everyday monotony and drudgery of housework or business dissipate as he/she focuses on the well worn words of a magical Jewish story that demands no concentration, no preparation – nothing but the teller's will to entertain.

You only have to look into the animated, sparkling eyes of an actor-parent, rabbi-parent, and/or workaday-parent in the midst of a "story session" with their children to realize that they have temporarily disconnected from reality and are soaring mightily in Storytelling Heaven.

And that, dear reader, is why the stories in this book exist.

Ostensibly, for your children.

But, in reality –

For you.

So, if you're an actor-parent, just think of the sound effects you can make when you read the Rosh Hashanah story, WAKE UP AND BEAT THE DRUMS! The banging and clanging will flow mightily – if you wish it – from your lips. The humor that arises from within this story will allow you to chuckle, laugh, even bellow heartily – something you may not have done for some time.

The Simchat Torah tale, DANCING WITH FIRE, will give you a renewed opportunity to kick up your feet – dance the mazurka if you desire – as you spin around and around, feeling the warmth of the story's circle of fire overhead.

As a rabbi-parent, you'll *kvell* as you pass on the famous HONI AND THE CAROB TREE story, gently stroking your 70 year old beard while feigning wide-eyed amazement at your new surroundings. You will have the opportunity to transform yourself – within two colorful pages – from a sarcastic youth filled with himself, to a thoughtful, sagacious old man who has learned a lesson in time, a lesson all those around you will eagerly applaud.

And if you're a workaday-parent, what more could you ask for than the Shabbat story, A TASTE OF PARADISE; a story that flows from the lips without effort and soothes even the most savage day like a refreshing verbal massage. After all, what could be more enjoyable than meeting our Jewish forefathers as they are called up to read from the Torah.

Of course, THE PERFECT PRESENT, will also fulfill your "think only calming thoughts" agenda. Ah! How you will luxuriate in the telling of this simple story that tugs at the heartstrings and creates wonderful images of no less a great personage than the "I'd do anything for you" lady of the house – Mother. Who else but Mom could create the Purim miracle found in this folk tale.

Ultimately, the stories in this book are what storytelling is all about. And as they help you weave their magic spell around your children, you will find – guaranteed! – that you too will become caught up in the act of telling. For these stories will quench your storytelling needs, at least temporarily, while providing a by-product all parents yearn for –

Happy children.

Rosh Hashanah
Wake Up And Beat The Drums!

It was almost Rosh Hashanah and all day long Nathan and Emily had been dreaming of eating apples dipped in honey. Their mouths watered as they smelled the challah and the chicken and the honey cake cooking in the oven.

They were all waiting for Mama to call out, "Time to come to the table everyone."

"So what does putting out a fire have to do with blowing the shofar on Rosh Hashanah?" Grandma Sarah asked, while Nathan and Emily climbed into her lap.

"Well, I'll tell you," continued Grandma Sarah. "But, you'll have to listen carefully to get the connection.

Once there was a poor Jewish farmer – a wise King Solomon he wasn't – who came to the big city for the very first time.

This farmer, Max, stayed with his distant cousin named Jacob. Each day Max would walk the streets of the big city and marvel at the buildings, the fancy clothes, the gadgets in the store windows, and the marketplace full of every kind of wonder.

In the middle of his last night in the city, Max was woken up by some very loud noises. "What's going on?" he called out.

"Go back to sleep," Jacob shouted. "A fire's broken out and those drums you hear are our fire alarm. No need to worry."

The next day, when Max returned to his village, he told everyone about the wonderful system in the big city. "When there's a fire, people beat on their drums and the fire burns out."

All the villagers decided that here in

their little village they should be up-to-date too.

They bought drums for every household. And a few weeks later, when a fire broke out in one of the village houses, everyone took out the drums and beat on them as loudly as they could. What a noise they made! But while they were beating and beating, the house burnt to the ground – every stick!

How could this be? Max wondered. And so did every other villager. Why didn't the marvelous system of the city work way out here in the country?

Luckily, there was an outsider in the village that day, passing through. "What is all this noise?" he asked Dovid, who worked behind the counter of the village's only grocery store. Actually, it was the only store altogether.

"People are beating the drums so the fire will go out," Dovid answered.

"Are you crazy? You can't put out a fire just by beating on some drums," said the out-of-towner in disbelief. "You only beat the drums so people will wake up and put out the fire with water hoses, blankets, sand, whatever they can find."

"But, Grandma," interrupted Nathan who was paying close attention to the story. "You haven't said anything about the shofar yet."

"Just wait. It's coming," said Grandma. "And here it is. The shofar is just like the drums. It's a call to wake up so that we can put out the fire. The shofar itself doesn't do that for us. We have to hear it, and think deep down where those fires could be that we have to put out, those things we have to do differently in the New Year."

"I see," said Nathan. "The shofar wakes us up, but we have to find out where the trouble is, and fix it ourselves."

"That's it!" said Grandma. "Exactly."

"I think Emily needs the shofar right now, Grandma," whispered Nathan.

"Is that so?" said Grandma.

"Yup," said Nathan, grinning. "She's fallen asleep. And she hasn't even tasted the apples and honey yet!"

NOW CONSIDER THIS:

✳ *What kind of feeling do you get when you hear the shofar on Rosh Hashanah?*

✳ *What do you think Grandma Sarah meant when she talked about "those fires"?*

✳ *Why do you think the villagers believed that the drums would put out the fire? Why do some people want to believe that the shofar will put out their fires too?*

Yom Kippur
The Secret Shofar Blasts

Don Fernando de Aguilar was a hidden Jew, a Marrano. There were many hidden Jews in Spain then, in the late 1500s, because of the anti-Jewish acts of the Inquisition. Don Fernando's choice was every Jew's choice in those times – to flee Spain or to become a Christian.

He and the other hidden Jews were not allowed to go to synagogue. Nor could they celebrate the Jewish holidays. They were forbidden to give their children lessons in Judaism. Everything they did as Jews was done with the utmost care and secrecy.

Now this same Don Fernando had a very important job as the conductor of the Royal Orchestra in Barcelona. Though he served the King and Queen with his music, he was still very much a Jew in his heart. And as the holiest day of the year, Yom Kippur, approached, Don Fernando and his closest Jewish friends planned secret services. The morning, afternoon and evening services were each held in a different place so as not to arouse suspicion. The Inquisitors had spies everywhere. The last service was to be in the basement of Don Manuel's leather shop.

The Marranos planned to fast, of course, and to gather their small group and sing the prayers. But one thing they could not do – could never do – was blow the shofar at the end of the service. Surely the great sounds of the shofar blasts would lead the Inquisitors right to their very door!

This year, more than anything, Don Fernando yearned to hear the shofar. He wanted his son Julio to hear it too. Julio was growing up so fast and might never hear the shofar blasts. Those blasts that had been heard through the centuries by all their ancestors, and had traveled to the very ears of the Holy One!

Don Fernando knew he had to do something, but what? Then he had an idea, which soon became a plan. He made an announcement that on a certain date, just after Yom Kippur, the Royal Orchestra would present a concert of the music of different lands. Posters about the concert were placed all over Barcelona. And whispers went from one hidden Jew to the next.

On that evening, after all their fasting and hiding and praying, whole families of hidden Jews came from all over Barcelona to the orchestra hall. So did Spanish families, merchants, commoners and noblemen alike. So did the Inquisitors themselves! The hall was full, every seat taken.

Don Fernando was nervous, yet he knew he had planned well. The orchestra played love songs from Italy and the dances of Arabia.

In the midst of these came the sounds of the shofar; the *teki'ah,* the *shevarim,* the *teru'ah.* The shofar blasts were woven in so carefully and expertly that even the leaders of the Inquisition heard them and suspected nothing. But all the hidden Jews who were there, Don Fernando's son Julio included, heard every single blast of the shofar, every single teki'ah, shevarim, and teru'ah, as if they were in the holiest of sanctuaries.

NOW CONSIDER THIS:

❋ *Why were the hidden Jews anxious to hear the shofar blasts?*

❋ *How do you think it felt to be a hidden Jew? What do you think the hidden Jews did to keep their Judaism alive?*

❋ *Why do you think the Jews had their services in different houses? How would you plan a secret service?*

Sukkot

Rabbi Zusya's Blanket

Before Rabbi Zusya was known to be the true *tzaddik* he was, he would travel from village to village to spread the joy of Torah. Once, during Sukkot, Rabbi Zusya appeared in the village synagogue of Ostrog. He looked poor and needy. Actually, he was poor and needy!

After services, one of the wealthy men of the town, Reb Shmuel, invited Zusya to stay in his *sukkah.* Of course, he thought Zusya was just any old beggar in need of a place to stay and food to eat for the holiday. He was soon to find out otherwise.

When it came time to sleep in the sukkah, Reb Shmuel lay down in one corner on his soft cushions piled high with pillows and blankets. As often happened to poor guests, Zusya slept in another corner, on the ground.

As time went by, however, the air grew chillier and chillier. After all, it

was fall. Zusya woke up and couldn't go back to sleep. He was so cold.

"Oh, please Holy One, Blessed One," Zusya prayed. "Zusya is a bit chilly. Could you send me just a little warmth?"

That very instant, a fire came down from On High and warmed the sukkah, but did not burn it. As quickly as it came, it disappeared.

Zusya fell fast asleep, but Reb Shmuel woke up. He was uncomfortably warm. He was also bewildered. Why was it so unseasonably warm in the sukkah? He looked around and saw nothing, shrugged his shoulders, threw off one of his covers, and went back to sleep.

Time passed. Zusya woke up feeling cold once again.

"Oh, please Holy One, Blessed One," he prayed. "Zusya is a little chilly. Could you send me just a bit of warmth? Just a little?"

Again the fire came from On High and warmed the sukkah, even more this time.

Zusya fell fast asleep, but Reb Shmuel woke up. "What is this?" he wondered out loud. "It feels like summer in here!" He looked around, saw nothing, shrugged his shoulders, and threw off another cover.

A little while later, Zusya grew cold again.

"Oh, please Holy one, Blessed One," he sang softly. "Zusya is a bit chilly. Could you send that warmth for Zusya?"

For a third time, the fire came and Zusya was comforted.

But Reb Shmuel was hotter than ever! "Now it feels like a steam bath in here," he muttered. This time he threw off all his covers, and when he looked around, he saw a tiny ball of fire flying all on its own through the branches of the sukkah roof towards the sky.

Suddenly, Reb Shmuel got up, worried that the fire would burn all the branches and leaves it passed and set fire to the whole sukkah. But nothing was even scorched.

It was then that he looked at his poor guest, this time with new eyes. "You don't need any covers, do you, Rabbi Zusya?" Reb Shmuel said. "You're covered and warmed by your prayers."

And from that time on, Zusya was always honored with the title "Rabbi Zusya" in the little town of Ostrog. He was recognized as the tzaddik he truly was. And Reb Shmuel never again put any guest, no matter how poor he seemed, on the bare floor of his sukkah to sleep!

NOW CONSIDER THIS:

✻ *Why do you think it was wrong for Reb Shmuel to put a guest on the bare floor? Where should he have put him?*

✻ *What do you think was unusual about the way Rabbi Zusya prayed?*

Simchat Torah
Dancing With Fire

The Baal Shem Tov and his students always gathered together for Simchat Torah. The students came from close by and far away. It was one of the happiest times of the year. Oh, to finish reading the Holy Scroll and start all over again! And to read about the end of Moses' life and how God created the world anew. To carry and dance with the scrolls in their arms and to parade seven times around the sanctuary! Why, they looked forward to this all year!

And this Simchat Torah was no different than any before. Maybe it was even merrier, for word had begun to spread through all the villages and cities around about the Baal Shem Tov and his teachings. Even more people had come. There was more singing and dancing, eating and drinking, than ever before.

Now Hannah, the Baal Shem Tov's wife, was full of the joy that Simchat Torah brought, too. But she had one little worry. She was watching the table that originally had been groaning with all her homemade cakes and wines, her noodle puddings, nuts and fruit. The table was now almost empty.

And even though it was very late, the students who were still there showed no signs of going home. No, if anything, their singing and dancing had grown louder and more joyful.

"Pssst!" Hannah opened the door to the courtyard and tried quietly to get her husband's attention. "Pssst."

The Baal Shem Tov saw her and came over.

"The food and wine I put out is almost gone," she whispered. "If I put out any more, we won't have enough for tomorrow when all these people will come again to pray and read the Torah, to sing and dance. You must tell them to stop and go home, then come back tomorrow."

The Baal Shem Tov listened carefully. "People serve God through all that they do: praying, studying, eating and drinking, too," he explained. "Whenever we eat or drink we know that what we are enjoying comes from God. But if you are worried, Hannah, then go in and tell them to stop. They will listen to you."

So Hannah stepped into the courtyard. She saw her husband's students dancing in a circle, arms linked.

Then she saw something else, something she had never seen before. Above their heads there was a canopy of sacred fire. Beautiful flames of red and yellow and blue danced with them in a circle too, burning no one and nothing.

Hannah quietly closed the door. She stood in the hallway for a moment. Then she smiled and, with a determined step, went into the kitchen to get more cakes and wines, noodle puddings and fruit, for all her honored guests.

NOW CONSIDER THIS:

✳ *Why do you think Hannah decided not to tell the students to go home?*

✳ *What are the things you like best about Simchat Torah?*

✳ *Why do you think there is a holiday that celebrates the reading of the end and the beginning of the Torah?*

Lost In The Woods

Mama hitched Soosie, the horse, to the wagon. "Miriam! Daniel!" she called. "Where are you? It's a long drive into town and Hanukkah starts tonight! Don't you remember?"

Miriam and Daniel tumbled out the doorway of the little white clapboard house. Of course they remembered!

"You don't want us to catch cold on the way, Mama!" said Miriam.

Only Miriam's eyes were visible. Everything else was covered up with scarves, hat, mittens, and a coat. Daniel too.

They waved to Papa who stood in the doorway. He was staying home with baby Leah. She had the sniffles. "Don't be long," he called out. "You know how tricky the weather can be this time of year."

"We'll be fine," Mama assured him.

All the way to town, Mama, Daniel and Miriam sang about *dreidles* and *latkes*. They even made up their own song to help them remember what Mama needed at the store.

We're going to get
*   potatoes and oil to fry,*
To make the best latkes
*   that money can buy.*
We'll get applesauce by
*   the jar or tin,*
And after we eat, our
*   dreidles we'll spin.*

Miriam and Daniel loved going to town, anytime. It didn't have to be Hanukkah. The general store was full of things to look at: barrels of flour and sugar, colorful fabrics, and wooden toys. And sometimes they saw their friends there.

Remembering Papa's advice, Mama

picked out what she needed as quickly as she could. "We have to go now, children," she said. "Don't forget the drive home and all we need to do."

On the trip home, Mama let Miriam and Daniel have some of the Hanukkah treats, the root beer and cherry candies. But when they were about halfway home, the sky suddenly grew very dark, even though it was the middle of the day.

Mama got a worried look on her face. She made clucking noises to Soosie. "Faster! Faster!"

Soon it was as dark as night, and snow and wind were whipping around them. They couldn't see anything, not even the road beneath the wagon.

"Don't worry," Mama said to comfort them. "Soosie knows her way home."

But Soosie slowed down, and slowed down some more.

"I don't think Soosie can see either," said Miriam.

"I'm cold," said Daniel, and he started to cry.

Mama didn't know which way to guide Soosie. Then Miriam sat up straight, pointing. "What's that, Mama?"

"It looks like a light," said Mama. There was hope in Mama's voice. "Come on," Mama clucked. She guided Soosie towards the light.

"Maybe it's Mr. Hendrick's house," said Mama. "Or the Grossingers."

The light grew bigger and bigger, though sometimes the snow was so thick they lost sight of it. That's when Mama would groan.

Finally, they could see that the light was shining in a window. When they reached it, they saw it wasn't just any light, but two candles shining in a menorah! Their menorah!

Papa ran out to meet them. "I was so worried," he said.

"*You* were worried!" Mama cried.

"I wasn't sure whether to light the menorah or wait for you," said Papa. "But lighting the candles felt right. It gave me hope."

"And saved us!" said Mama. "A miracle! You don't know...."

"A Hanukkah miracle!" said Miriam.

"Let's make the latkes," said Daniel, who wasn't frightened anymore.

NOW CONSIDER THIS:

✻ *What Hanukkah miracle do you know about?*

✻ *What kind of feeling do you get when you light the menorah with your family?*

✻ *Have you ever been lost or think you were lost?*
What helped you to find your way home?

Honi And The Carob Tree

One morning, Honi, who lived in Israel, went for a walk to enjoy the beauty of God's world. He passed an especially well-tended garden where he noticed a very old man bent over a sapling.

"Shalom," Honi greeted the man. "What are you planting?"

"A carob tree," the man answered, still digging the hole for the sapling.

Honi could picture the hard sweet pods that grew on the carob tree behind his house. That tree had been there for as long as he could remember.

"But it will take a long time for this tree to grow and bear fruit," Honi said.

"Seventy years," said the old man.

"Seventy years!" echoed Honi, amazed. "Well, then you won't live to taste the carob's fruit."

"No, I won't. But perhaps my children and certainly my children's children will. I am doing this for them. How else will they be able to enjoy its fruit?"

"Maybe you should plant some strawberries instead," Honi joked.

The old man shrugged and smiled. "One day, you will see."

Honi continued on his walk, enjoying the warmth of the sun, when he saw a large rock by the side of the road. He sat down on it for a little rest and, before he realized it, he fell asleep. This wasn't an ordinary sleep, however, for Honi slept and slept and slept. While he slept, the bushes and grass around him grew and grew until he was hidden from view.

When Honi finally awoke, he did not realize how long he had slept. He did wonder at the long white beard where his much shorter brown one had once been. And he wondered at the stiffness he felt when he stood up, and at all the grass that covered him.

Perhaps I am still dreaming, he thought.

Honi rushed home, eager to hear

what his family would say about his strange sleep and this long beard. He tugged on it. Could it be real?

Honi stumbled onto the path which had grown wider than he remembered. And it was so much busier than he remembered, with carts and people, cows and squawking chickens.

Honi felt more bewildered than ever. He passed many houses he did not recognize. At last he came to a familiar garden, still beautiful and well-tended.

Ah, this is where that old man was planting a carob tree before I fell asleep, he thought.

Honi peered into the garden. But instead of a sapling, there stood a great wide carob tree, its pods heavy on the branches. A young girl played underneath, jumping up to touch the pods and make them fall.

"Shalom," Honi said to the girl.

She turned around to see who called her.

"The old man who planted this tree, is he home?" Honi asked.

The girl looked puzzled. "I have never seen him," she answered. "My grand-father was a small boy when *his* grandfather planted this tree. Would you like a pod?" she asked, handing him one of the carob pods. "They're tasty when you bite into them."

I have been sleeping for seventy years, thought Honi. And then the old man's words came back to him as clearly as if he had heard them that very day.

"I am doing this for my children and my children's children. How else will they be able to enjoy the fruit? One day, you will see."

"Yes, old man," Honi said out loud, startling the little girl. "You were right. I do see."

And he knew at that moment that he would take this little girl's carob and plant the seeds, just as the old man had done, for his children and his children's children.

NOW CONSIDER THIS:

✳ *What is the lesson Honi learned?*

✳ *If you fell asleep for 70 years, what do you think the world would look like when you awoke?*

✳ *What other story do you know about Honi?*

(See Ten Classic Jewish Children's Stories by Peninnah Schram)

Purim
The Perfect Present

Soon it would be Purim and everyone in Pinsk would give gifts to everyone else. On his way home from school, Shlomo worried about what he would give his teacher, Reb Yitz. All the other boys would be giving their gifts to him tomorrow. But Shlomo and his mother did not have much money to spend.

When Shlomo walked into the house, he knew something was wrong. His mother stood there frowning. "I work so hard, Shlomo, and you forget the firewood, the chickens, the eggs."

"I'm sorry, Mama. I was thinking about a present for Reb Yitz."

"Presents? Who has time for presents? You need to fetch the wood!"

So Shlomo ran to the forest at the edge of town to collect sticks for the fire.

He stopped to look at one stick that seemed good for carving and leaned against a tree, reaching into his pocket for his knife.

He thought about Purim and the story of brave Queen Esther and wicked Haman, silly King Ahashvayrosh and kind Mordecai.

"Reb Yitz is brave like Esther and kind like Mordecai," Shlomo thought. "I'll carve both."

So he whittled the beautiful face of Queen Esther on one side of the wood and the kindly face of her cousin Mordecai on the other.

But before he could carve more, he felt the darkness around him closing in.

"I'll have to finish this later, after I do my chores. Oh, no! My chores!"

Quickly he gathered the firewood and his carving and ran home.

"Where have you been?" his mother asked as soon as she saw him.

"I started a present for Reb Yitz. See?" He held up his carving.

"Oh, Shlomo. The chickens eat grain, not puppets. There is so much work to do."

As Shlomo did his chores, he worried. There was so little time left.

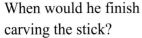

When would he finish carving the stick?

When Shlomo woke early the next morning, he went to the bench where he had placed his carving, but it wasn't there! He looked everywhere. Then the crackling noise of the fire startled him. His mother was feeding the fire in the next room. He felt his eyes filling with tears. Could his mother be so angry with him that she would throw his carving into the fire? he wondered.

He ran to the fireplace and then he saw it. The carving was propped proudly on the mantle, but it looked different. Esther wore a flowery red dress and a scarf on her head, and Mordecai was dressed in a blue robe and black satin hat! The carving had become a puppet with clothes that were carefully joined as if the two characters were really one.

"Mother! I can't believe you did this!" Shlomo stammered, joyfully.

"Me? Would I have time to do such things?"

"But...."

"It must be like it was for Aunt Gertel those weeks Uncle Pinchas was sick," his mother said.

"You mean those mornings when Aunt Gertel opened the door and found a pile of firewood all neatly stacked? She said it was a miracle."

His mother nodded. "Yes, a miracle. Now get dressed and you can take the puppet to Reb Yitz."

As Shlomo lifted the puppet, he noticed a familiar smell like the herbs that dried in the kitchen in the fall. Then he remembered and went over to his mother's trunk in the corner. When he opened it, the same sweet fragrance surrounded him. On top lay an old red flowered scarf which matched the puppet's red skirt, but the scarf was no longer whole. Someone had cut off a large corner. He knew then that it was his mother who had sewn the puppet's clothes. He couldn't help smiling. Maybe it was also his mother who stacked Aunt Gertel's firewood. His tired, working-so-hard mother, who had no time, had found time to work miracles for others.

NOW CONSIDER THIS:

❋ *Who are some other characters in the Purim story besides those mentioned in this story? What part did they play in the story?*

❋ *Why did Shlomo and the other boys want to give a gift to Reb Yitz on Purim? What are some other customs about Purim?*

❋ *Why do you think that Shlomo's mother performed "miracles" without telling anyone?*

Passover
Elijah's Cup

Yudel grew up in a small town in Poland and loved to listen to the stories the *shochet,* the butcher, told the children who wandered into his shop. One day, after telling a story about the Prophet Elijah, the shochet surprised Yudel by looking right at him and saying, "Whatever you do, Yudel, never change your name. It comes from the Yiddish word meaning Jew. As long as you are Yudel, you will never forget you are a Jew."

Yudel, of course, agreed to this strange request, though he was bewildered by it. Soon enough he would realize the importance of the shochet's words. A few weeks later, as was true of so many poor boys then, Yudel was taken from his home and family to serve in the Russian army.

During his long years as a Russian

soldier, there were many times Yudel was tempted to change his name. Life would have been so much easier for him. No extra duties, no name calling, no little kicks and shoves – no big ones either. But he always remembered the shochet's words and kept his name.

On one bitter winter evening, when Yudel was on sentry duty, a soldier walked by and said in Yiddish, "Do you know Yudel, this is the first night of Passover."

Yudel turned around to take a better look at this soldier who spoke Yiddish. Wasn't he the only Jewish soldier for miles? But the man had vanished.

The soldier's words haunted Yudel, and a longing came over him. He desperately wanted to recite the *Haggadah,* but he couldn't remember even one word of it. He prayed and prayed – *Just let me remember one word!*

And that's when a word did come to him. He remembered the first words of the question he had sung at the *Seder* table when he was a little boy, *Mah-nishtanah.* "How is this night different?" Then the whole question suddenly came to him: "How is this night different than all other nights?"

Yudel's heart filled with joy at the long lost yet familiar words. One word led to another, and there he was on guard duty, marching up and down the lonely path in the snow, singing the whole Haggadah as if he were at his own family's table. The words warmed him like the hot soup his mother had always served at the Seder.

That night, his sentry duty over, Yudel got ready for bed, the words of the Haggadah still filling his head. He looked at the little table by his mattress. It looked so empty – not like the holiday table at home with its piles of matzah, the Seder Plate, his mother's wonderful dishes of potatoes and chicken, carrots and raisins. Then he remembered the cup

of wine for Elijah that always stood in the very center of the table.

"I don't have matzah or a Seder Plate or wine," he thought, "but I do have a cup." And he put it right in the center of the little table to remind him of the Seder Table at home and the shochet's stories, and, of course, the Prophet Elijah.

Yudel dreamt he was watching Elijah that night, and when he awoke in the morning, he looked over at the table and the cup. Something glimmered in it. He stood up and peered in. He saw that his cup was filled with wine! Yudel smiled. Could it be that instead of drinking wine from a cup, as he usually did, Elijah had actually filled his instead?

From then on, Yudel's days were full of thoughts of this Passover miracle. When, at last, he was released from the army and went back to his little town, he headed straight to the shochet's shop to tell him the whole story. The shochet didn't seem at all surprised, though. Somehow, he had known all along.

NOW CONSIDER THIS:

❊ *Why do you think the shochet told Yudel that if he remembered his name he would always be a Jew?*

❊ *How was Yudel's night different than all his other nights?*

❊ *What's your favorite part of the Seder?*

Shavuot
A King's Love

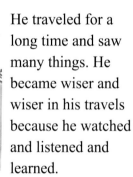

Grandma, do you have a story for us?" asked Nathan as he followed Grandma Sarah to the living room. His little sister Emily trailed behind.

"Of course, I have a story," said Grandma Sarah. "Do you know what a king has to do with the Torah?"

It was Shavuot, and Nathan and Emily were stuffed full of blintzes. Grandma too. Blintzes filled with cottage cheese and cinnamon. Blintzes filled with blueberry jam and topped with sour cream. They were so stuffed, they couldn't even really walk. They waddled.

"Does the story have blintzes in it?" said Nathan.

"No, no blintzes," said Grandma Sarah. "Just listen.

Once there was a king who went searching for a kingdom that needed a ruler.

He traveled for a long time and saw many things. He became wiser and wiser in his travels because he watched and listened and learned.

One day he entered a land where the city walls were crumbling, the fields were brown and dry, and the houses were in disrepair. He took out his horn and called all the people together in the marketplace.

"I would like to be your king. I will rule over you wisely and with care," he said.

"Why should we listen to you?" they answered. "Why should we believe you? We don't even know you."

The king heard the people and the very next day he got to work. He rebuilt the city walls, stone by stone. He set up channels for water to run into the fields and turn them from brown to a lush green. He went from house to house, painting and fixing. Little by little, people from the kingdom came to help him in his work.

And each week, when he bought his supplies in the market-place, he stopped to chat with the egg seller and the farmer and the baker. When he stayed in the inns for his lodging and food, he heard from this one and that one about all their troubles or their joyous celebrations.

Finally, after many months had passed, he once again took out his horn and called the people together.

"I would like to be your king," he told them. "I will rule over you wisely, and with care."

This time the people responded with loud cheering.

"If that's the end, Grandma," interrupted Nathan, *"you haven't said a thing about the Torah."*

"I know, I know. Where's the fire?" said Grandma Sarah. *"I was just getting to that part.*

"Just like the King did all these things for the people of that land so they would trust him and accept his rules, so God did for us. God brought us out of Egypt, split the Red Sea for us, and sent manna to feed us. Then we were ready to accept and trust God and God's laws, the Torah. See, that's where it comes in!"

"And that's what we remember today," said Nathan getting excited. *"On Shavuot, we remember how we got the Torah on Mount Sinai!"*

"Absolutely!" said Grandma Sarah. *"What a good memory you have."*

"But I think Emily is remembering something else right now, Grandma," said Nathan quietly.

"What is that?" said Grandma Sarah.

"Blintzes," said Nathan grinning.

They both looked at Emily who was fast asleep in Grandma Sarah's lap, a smile on her face and her hand resting on her tummy.

NOW CONSIDER THIS:

✽ *How are the Jewish people like the people in this story, and how is God like the king? What are the differences?*

✽ *What happened on Mount Sinai? What are some of the commandments the Jewish people received on Mount Sinai?*

✽ *What rules would you make if you were a king?*

A Taste Of Paradise

One summer, Tamar and Efraim rented a cabin in the mountains to enjoy the fresh country air. It was Friday afternoon, all their Shabbat preparations were done, and they decided to go for a walk in the woods before candlelighting. The woods seemed more alive than ever with birds and insects and little scurrying creatures.

"See how they hurry to welcome the Shabbat Queen?" Tamar said.

Efraim smiled and took her hand, and they wandered happily.

Suddenly Tamar gasped. "Efraim," she said, "where's the path we were following?"

Efraim looked down. Under his feet were grass and moss and little flowers – but no path. "We must find our way back quickly," he said.

They turned around and searched for the path.

"Does this look familiar?" said Tamar.

"I'm afraid not," answered Efraim. "We're lost. And Shabbat is coming. We won't be able to find the path in the dark."

"We must pray," said Tamar. And they did, while the woods grew darker and darker around them. Then Tamar heard something. "Did you hear that too, Efraim?" she asked.

They both turned and saw a woman walking toward them. She was dressed plainly but had a lovely glow to her face and hair. "Excuse me," said Efraim. "We're lost. We'd like to find our cabin. Could you help us?"

"My name is Rachel," said the woman. "I don't know where your cabin is, but you may join us for Shabbat. However, one thing I must ask of you is that you do not say a word, nor ask any questions. No matter what you see."

Efraim and Tamar agreed.

That night passed like a dream.

They found themselves in a synagogue built within a magnificent palace. The singing to welcome the Shabbat bride made them feel as if they were floating above the ground; they were lifted so high.

Then there was the Shabbat evening meal and more singing. Tamar and Efraim didn't need to worry about saying anything. They were speechless with the wonder of it all.

That night they slept the sleep of those who are young and have no cares.

In the morning, they knew this was no dream, for they awoke in the same magnificent palace. They were led back to the synagogue for the morning service. Tamar and Efraim found it much harder to keep quiet now. They were full of questions: *Where were they? Who were these people?* But since they wanted to stay, they kept their questions to themselves.

Soon the time came for the reading of the Torah. When it was lifted from the ark, the Torah scroll looked as if it were blazing with fire. But it couldn't be. No one who held it was burned! Tamar and Efraim's mouths dropped open, yet not a peep came out.

Then those honored to come up to the Torah were called. The first name Efraim and Tamar heard was, "Our Teacher, Moses son of Amram."

Then they heard, "David the King" called. Then, "Solomon the King." They could hardly contain themselves with the calling of each name. Could it be that they were actually celebrating Shabbat with *The* Moses and *The* David and *The* Solomon of the Torah!

When "Our Father Abraham" was called, they could keep quiet no longer. Cries of amazement and joy leapt from their mouths.

All at once, the palace disappeared. Tamar and Efraim were left standing in the kitchen in their own little cabin with the table all set for the coming Shabbat. They looked at each other's glowing face, and smiled. From then on, each Shabbat tasted so *so* sweet, like gifts from the World To Come.

NOW CONSIDER THIS:

✳ *Why do you think Tamar and Efraim weren't allowed to say anything? How did their words affect what was happening around them?*

✳ *What makes Shabbat special for you?*

✳ *Why do you think the Rabbis call Shabbat "A Taste Of Paradise"?*